Mel Bay's Instrumental Caroling Book

By William Bay

For:

Violin	Cornet
Flute	Baritone Horn T.C.
Trumpet	Baritone Horn B.C.
Guitar	E♭ Clarinet
Clarinet	Alto Clarinet
Alto Sax	Baritone Sax
Tenor Sax	Bassoon
Trombone	Cello
Bass Clarinet	String Bass

Instrumental Caroling Book

Enclosed is a collection of favorite Christmas hymns, carols, and songs. Each song is arranged for C instruments, Bb instruments, Eb instruments, and bass clef instruments. In addition, a special flute part is included in the range which is comfortable for that particular instrument. The harmonizations correspond with those found in major hymnals; and, therefore, instruments may play out of this book in worship celebrations with congregational singing, choirs, organ, piano, and other instruments. In addition, each song has been arranged with a melody and harmony part.

It is hoped that this book will enable a wide variety of instruments to participate meaningfully in caroling and worship experiences to celebrate this joyous season.

Instrumental Part Guide

C PART—Violin, Guitar

FLUTE PART—Flute

Bb PART—Clarinet, Bass Clarinet, Cornet/Trumpet, Tenor Saxophone, Baritone Horn Treble Clef

Eb PART—Alto Saxophone, Baritone Saxophone, Eb Clarinet, Alto Clarinet

BASS CLEF PART—Trombone, Bassoon, Baritone Horn Bass Clef, Cello, String Bass

Contents

Silent Night, Holy Night

What Child Is This

What Child Is This

Angels From The Realms Of Glory

6

Angels From The Realms Of Glory

Angels From The Realms Of Glory

The First Noel

8

The First Noel

Let All Mortal Flesh Keep Silence

Let All Mortal Flesh Keep Silence

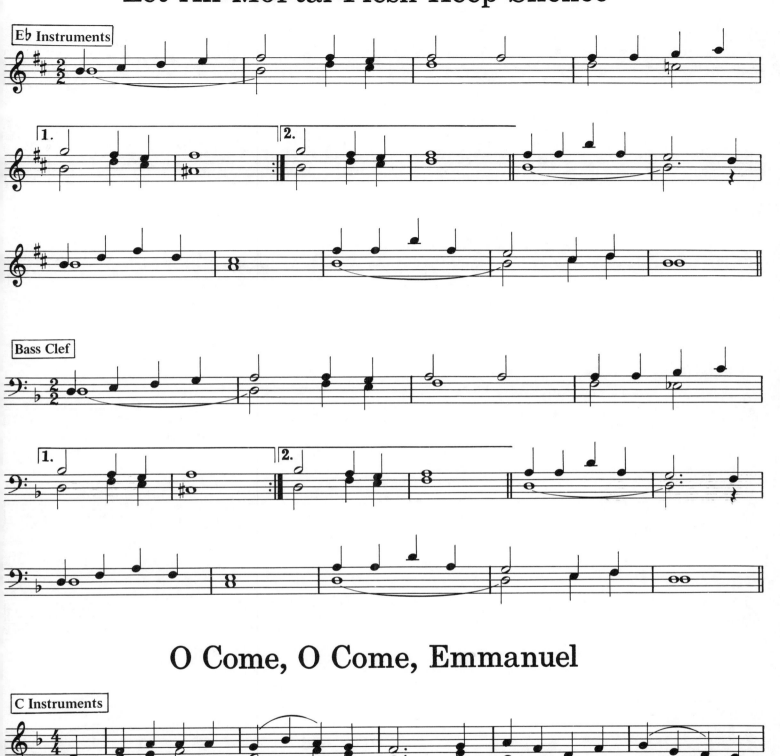

O Come, O Come, Emmanuel

O Come, O Come, Emmanuel

O Come, O Come, Emmanuel

O Come, All Ye Faithful

O Come, All Ye Faithful

Hark! The Herald Angels Sing

Away In A Manger

Away In A Manger

Angels We Have Heard On High

Angels We Have Heard On High

O Little Town Of Bethlehem

19

O Little Town Of Bethlehem

O Little Town Of Bethlehem

Bass Clef

As With Gladness, Men Of Old

C Instruments

Flute

B♭ Instruments

As With Gladness, Men Of Old

Good Christian Men, Rejoice

Good Christian Men, Rejoice

God Rest You Merry, Gentlemen

God Rest You Merry, Gentlmen

Lift Up Your Heads, Ye Mighty Gates

Lift Up Your Heads, Ye Mighty Gates

Bb Instruments

Eb Instruments

Bass Clef

Coventry Carol

C Instruments

Flute

Coventry Carol

Bb Instruments

Eb Instruments

Bass Clef

We Three Kings

C Instruments

27

We Three Kings

Flute

Bb Instruments

Eb Instruments

We Three Kings

It Came Upon A Midnight Clear

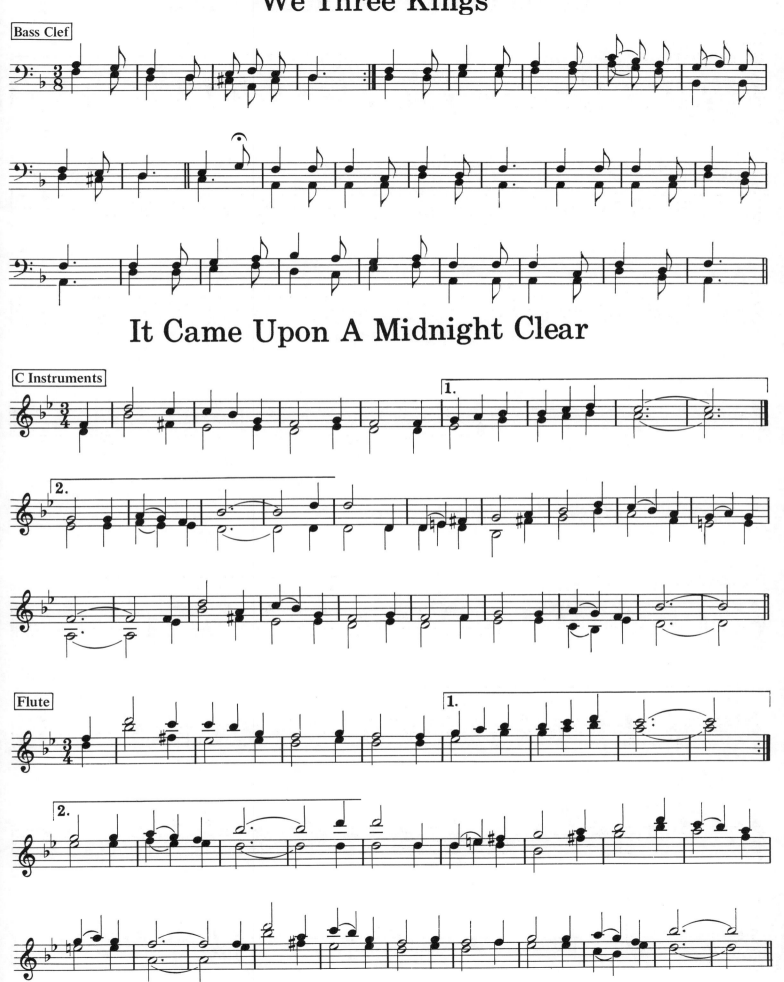

29

It Came Upon A Midnight Clear

It Came Upon A Midnight Clear

We Wish You A Merry Christmas

We Wish You A Merry Christmas

Jingle Bells

Jingle Bells

Jingle Bells

Rosa Mystica
(Lo How A Rose)

35

Rosa Mystica
(Lo How A Rose)

Deck The Halls

Deck The Halls

Joy To The World

Joy To The World

Flute

B♭ Instruments

E♭ Instruments

Bass Clef

Great Music at Your Fingertips